It Starts With A Canvas

Featuring the artwork of
Michelle Head

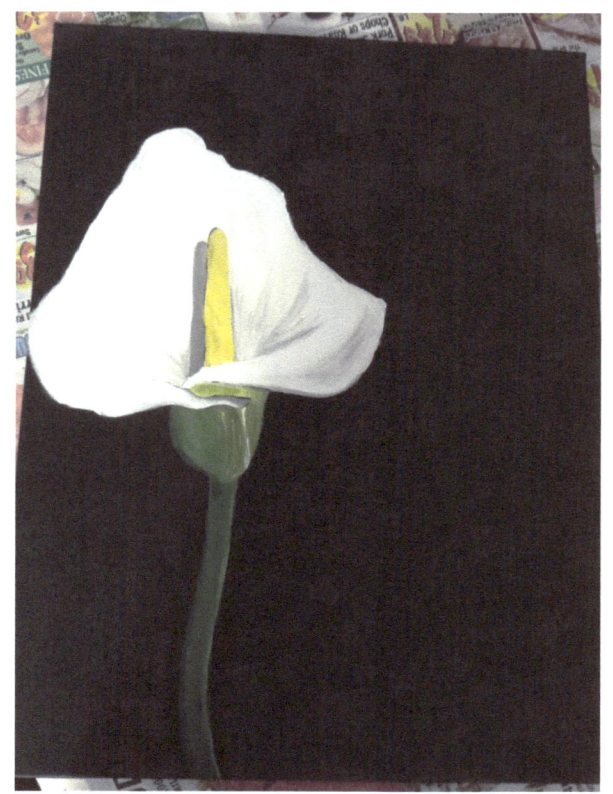

by

Bradley Zink

ISBN: **1515112527**
ISBN-13: **978-1515112525**

DEDICATION

Art is a crucial and integral part of our childrens' education. I would like to dedicate this book to ALL of the children who strive and desire to learn the "arts", and who work and develop to become our Future leading Artists. I also dedicate this book to artists like Michelle Head, who help to inspire our children.

"Aspire To Inspire"

ACKNOWLEDGMENTS

I would like to thank Michelle Head, for offering to share her magnificent work with me, to not only bring to the world a glimpse of her incredible talent, but for participating in this book to help Save the Arts in Our Schools.

The first programs to be cut from school, sadly is the Music and Arts. With the help of artists, such as Michelle, and with 75% of the proceeds going back to the schools, perhaps we can help to develop and inspire all of our Future Artists

About the Artist

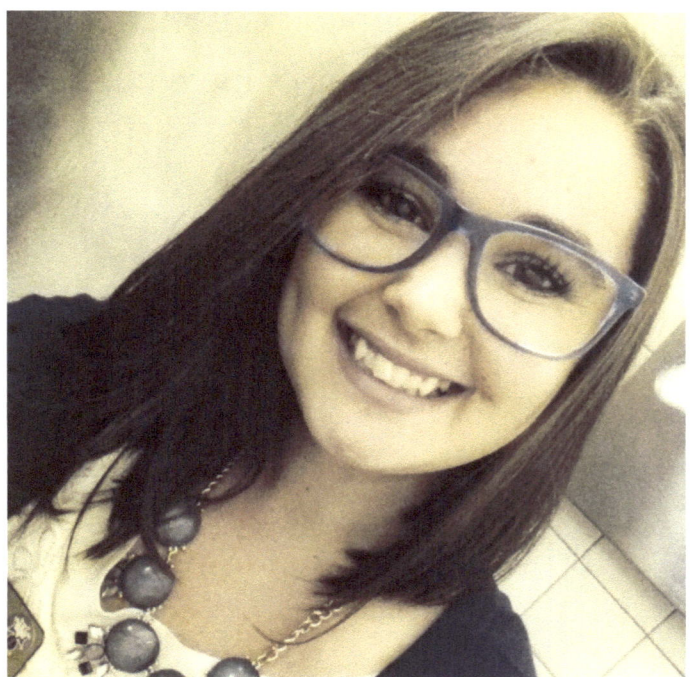

Michelle Head

I was born in San Clemente California to two wonderful people, Michael and AnnaMarie Head. Shortly after I was born, we moved to Oceanside California, welcomed my sister Katie, and then moved to San Marcos California and welcomed my brother Brian. We have been in San Marcos ever since.

I was born and raised Catholic. My grandparents, Joseph and Carrol Sposato are the reason for that. They are my everything. Besides my parents that is. A little over two years ago they moved in with us so that we could take care of them. I dropped classes at school so that I could stay home and care for them. I wouldn't have changed that for anything. They were my world. A lot I do now I dedicate to them. My cooking, my drawing, my praying.

I have played soccer since I was 4 years old. I still play. I am 21 years old now. Soccer has been my main hobby for many years. Between tournaments and practices, there was not much time for anything else.

Once the 7th grade hit my life changed forever. In February of 2007 I found out that I have Type 1 Diabetes. Not something easily stomached. My pancreas doesn't make insulin and my body cannot control my blood sugar because of that. It I something I struggle with every day. That is why I have taken and put so much time in to drawing. It is a way for me to express how I am feeling. That is especially why I took to the zentangles. Through each little detail you can see how I am feeling. The harsh lines are representation of a rough mood, while the softer lines represent a good or easy-going mood. I don't do much color because I better express myself in black and white. Color seems to just fluster my brain. I go back to it every once in a while but I feel I'm not good with colors.

I like to paint. Not often. But I do like it. I love painting flowers. I like to think that is all thanks to my grandfather. He spent so much time taking care of his flowers and I appreciated that so much. My mom is that way now.

I am a very grateful person. All of my family is so close. I love being able to spend time with my living grandparents. They are wonderful and such fun personalities to be around. Then there is my aunt. I love her like crazy. Her and her husband and all 3 of their kids. I babysit for them a lot and Grace, the eldest child of theirs, loves to color and I spend time with her coloring in coloring book. I have made her maps and things of that sort for her birthdays. I'd like to think of her as my little protégé but who knows.

I can't go without noticing my brother and sister. Through everything they have been there for me and helped in ways I can't even explain. No matter what, I know they will always be there for me. They even still support me at soccer games.

Last but not least, I have the most amazing boyfriend. We have been together a little over 4 years and I can honestly say I am blessed. Every struggle, every up, and every down he has been y my side. He helps when I feel I don't need it. He has helped me stay on top of Diabetes. He has driven me to soccer games and helped mend my injuries. He is my rock and has been one of my biggest supporters for art. He keeps encouraging me to do and try to put my name out there. If it wasn't for him and my mom I probably would have given up on art.

I am so glad I didn't ☺

Another interesting fact, I love wheel of fortune. I guess almost every puzzle and am very competitive with whomever I am watching the show with.

I love to bake. I love to experiment and try to create my own desserts and then hare with everyone. I loved cooking and baking for my grandparents. When they lived with us I tried to make them dinner when I could. To see their faces light up made everything worth it.

I have 3 dog at home, 1 bird, and various fish. I love animals. I rescue them every time I see them running around. I always feel bad when I see commercials about abandoned animals.

I can make clothes. I go in to that a couple months back. I made myself some skirts and scarves and shirts. My next goal is to make pants. Need to even out the legs.

I really just love to draw. I draw on everything. Menus at restaurants, napkins, books, notes, random papers, my actual sketch pads…etc. ☺

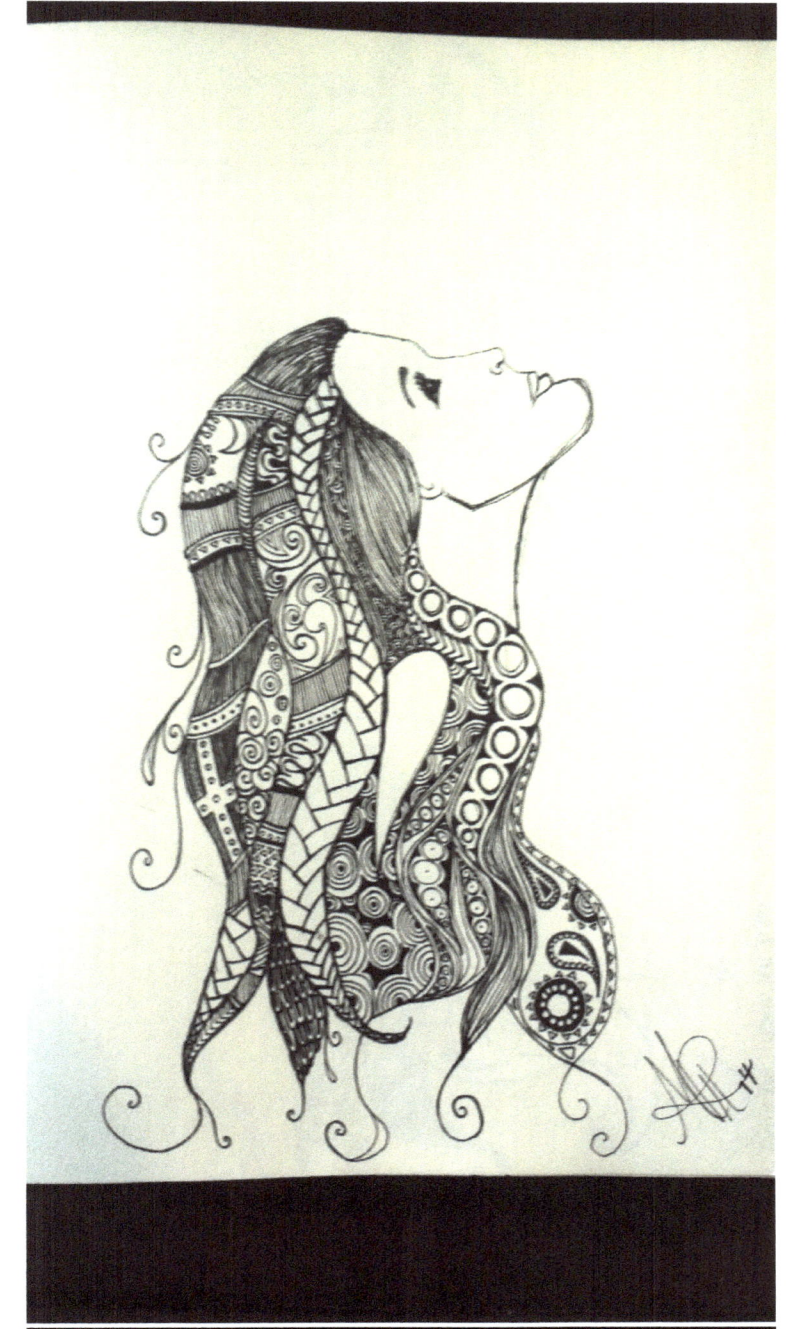

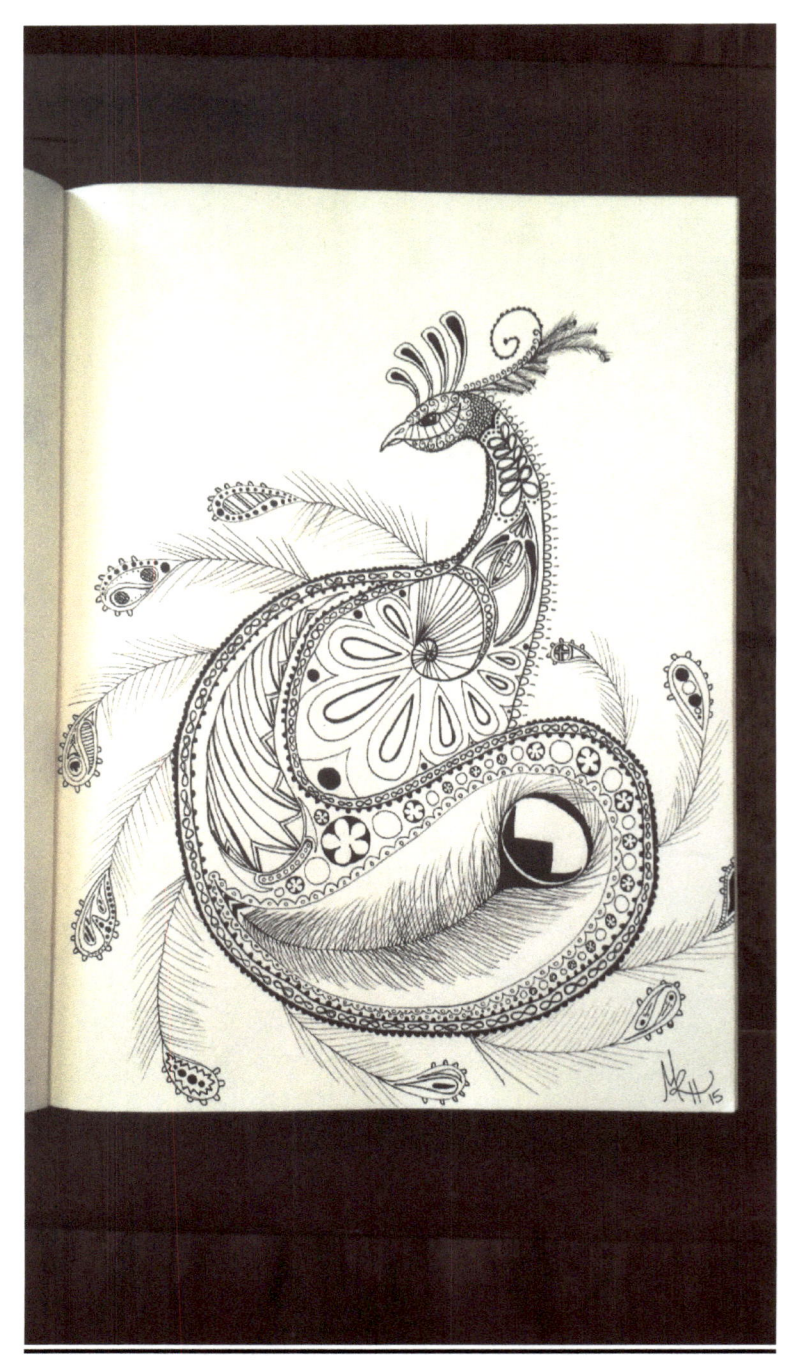

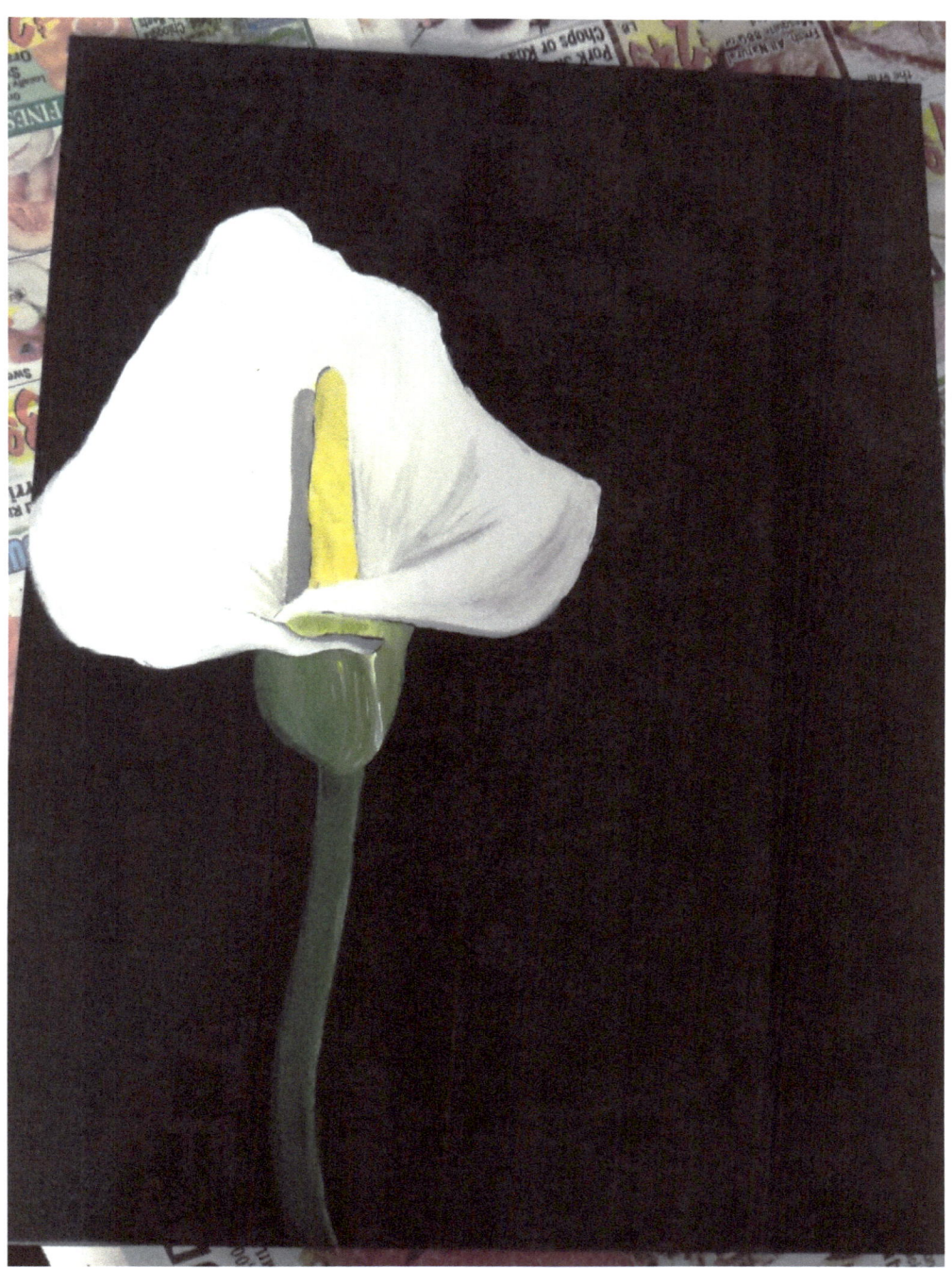

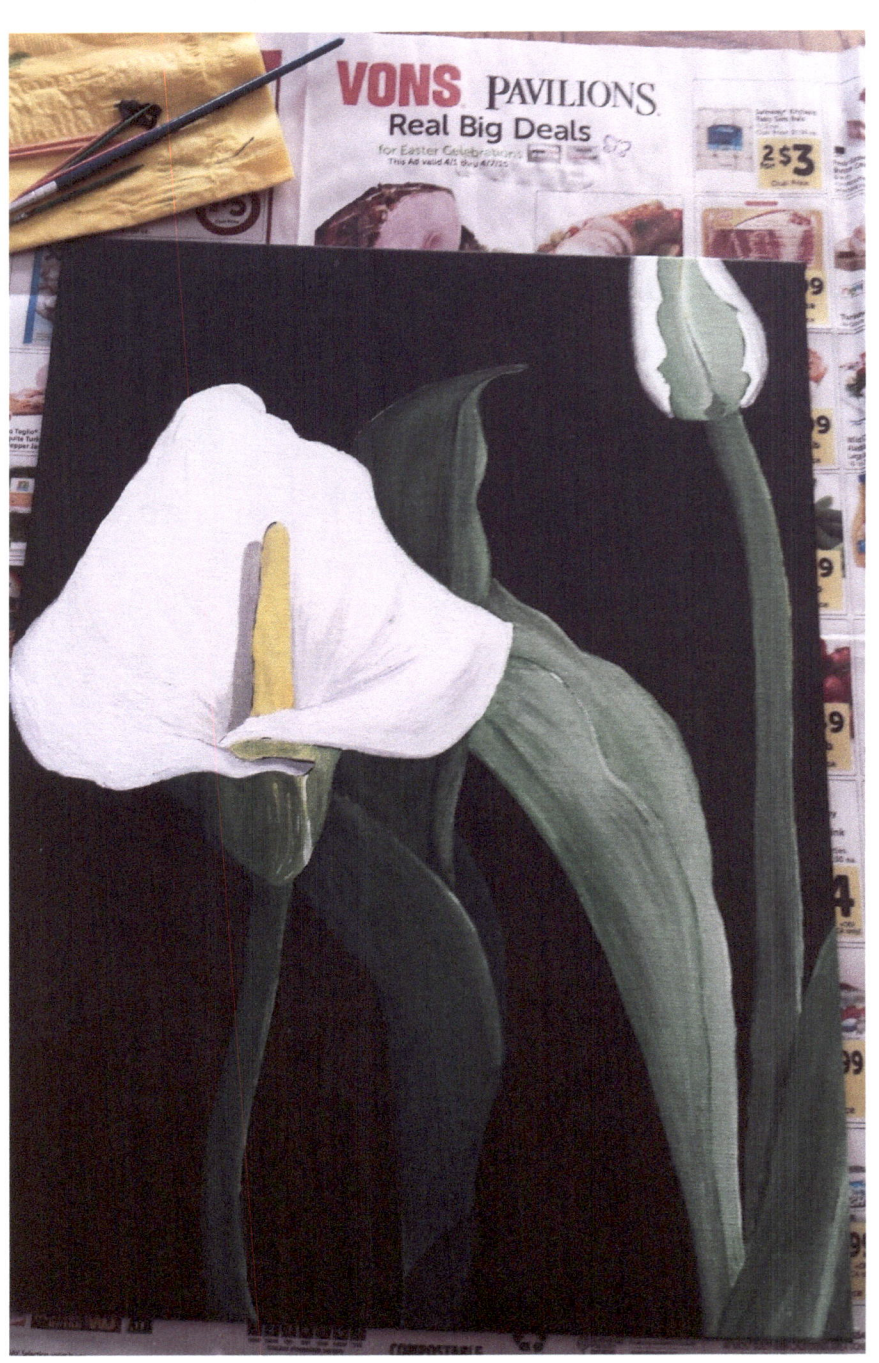

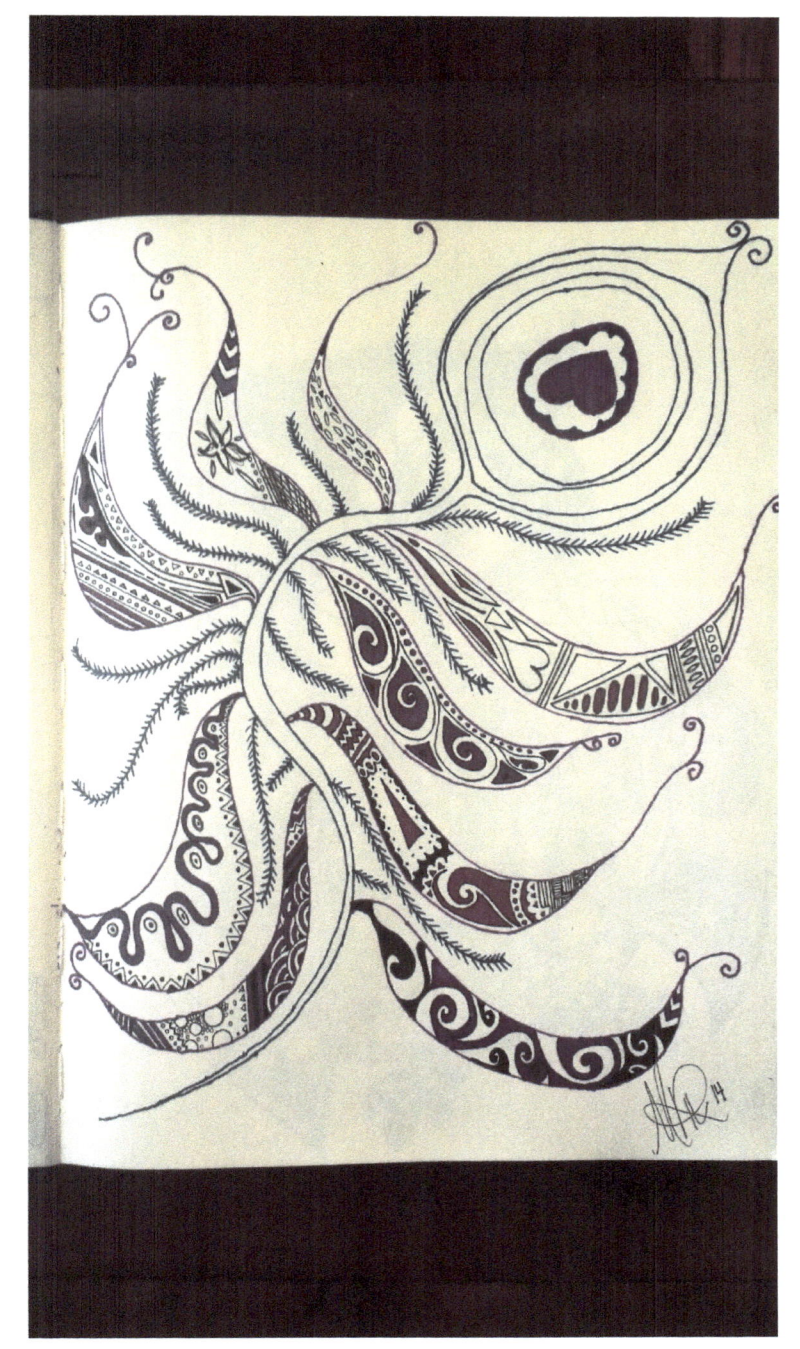

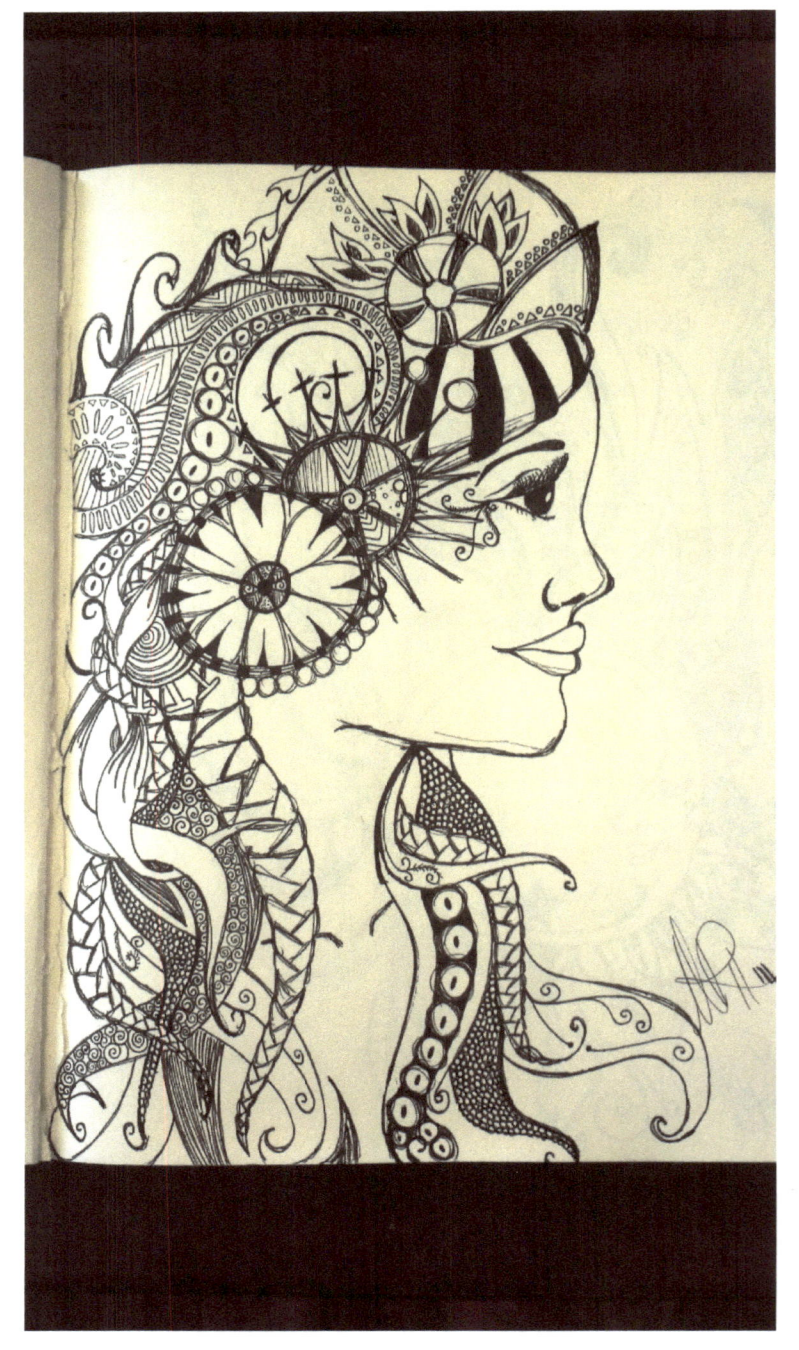

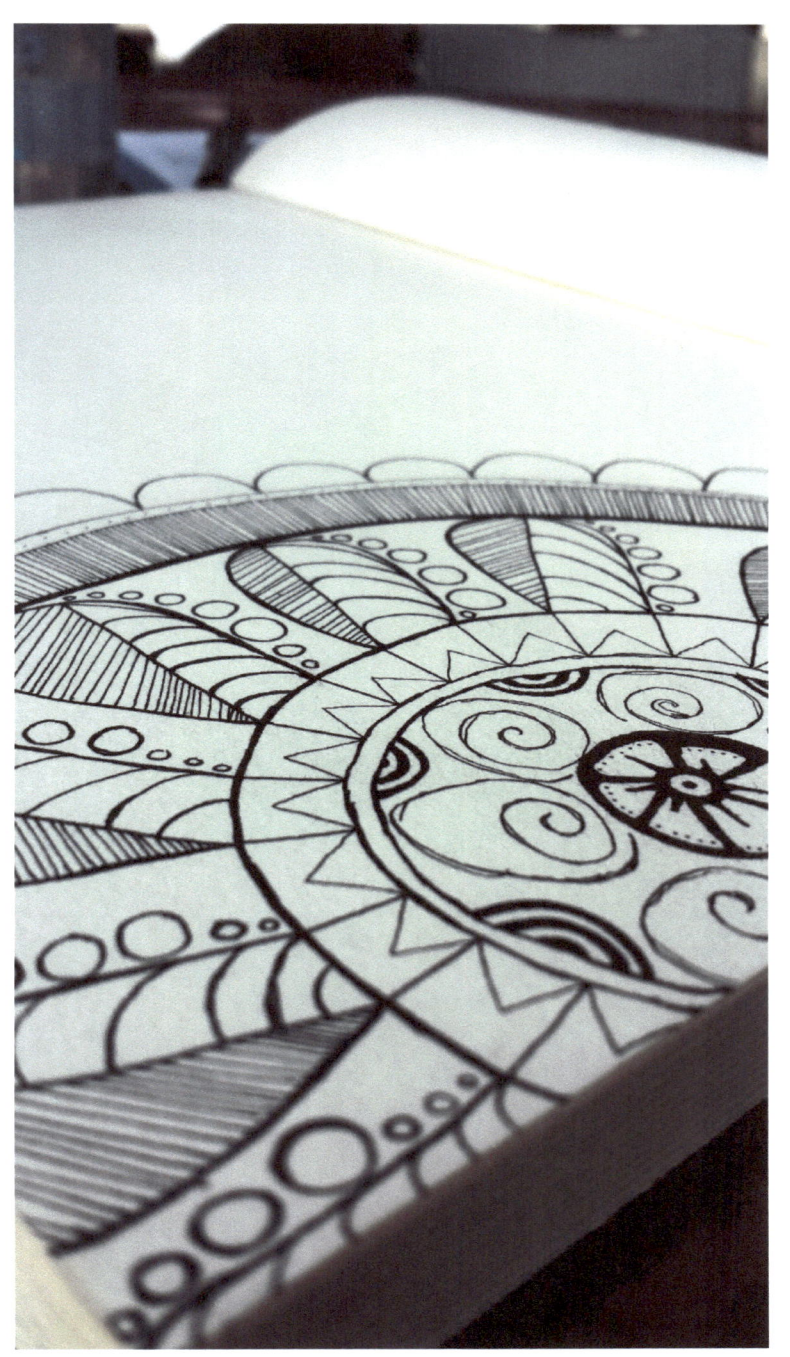

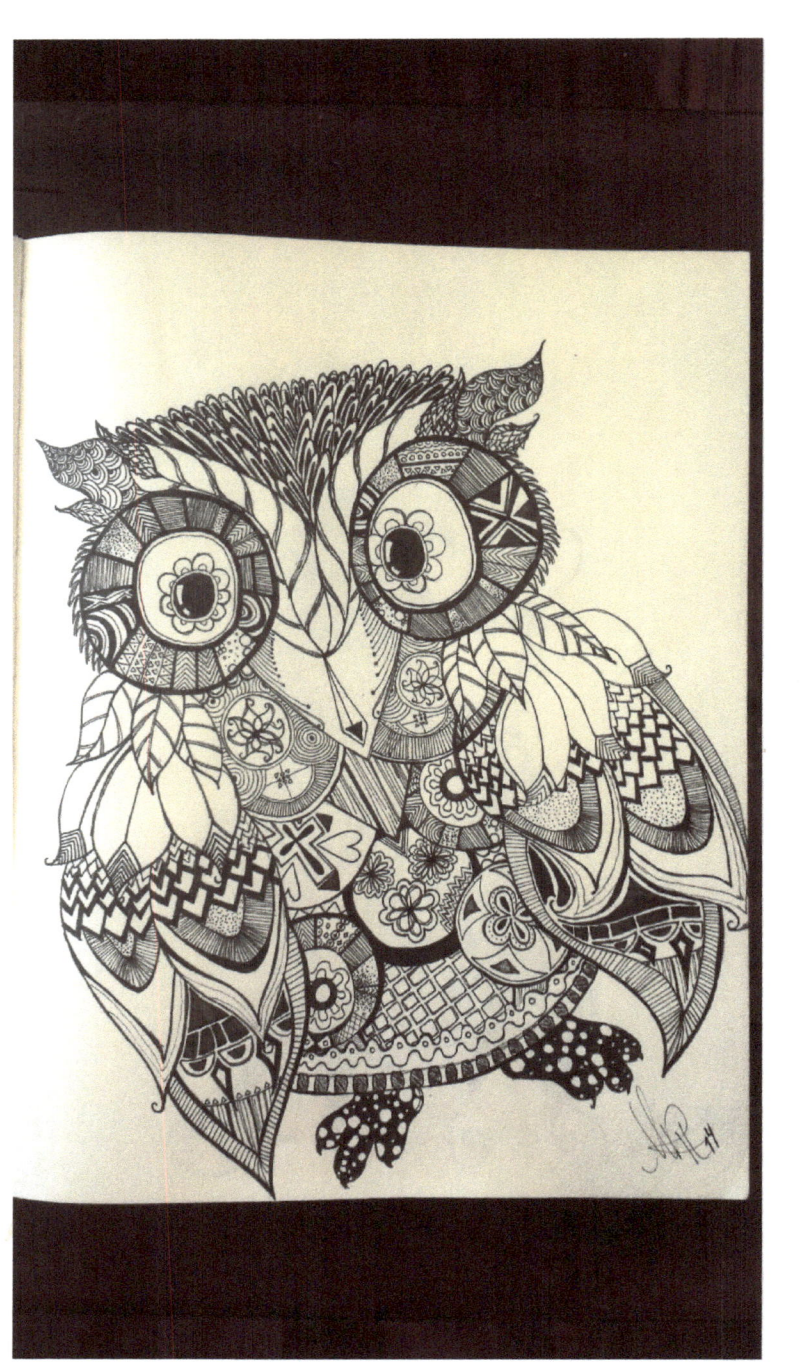

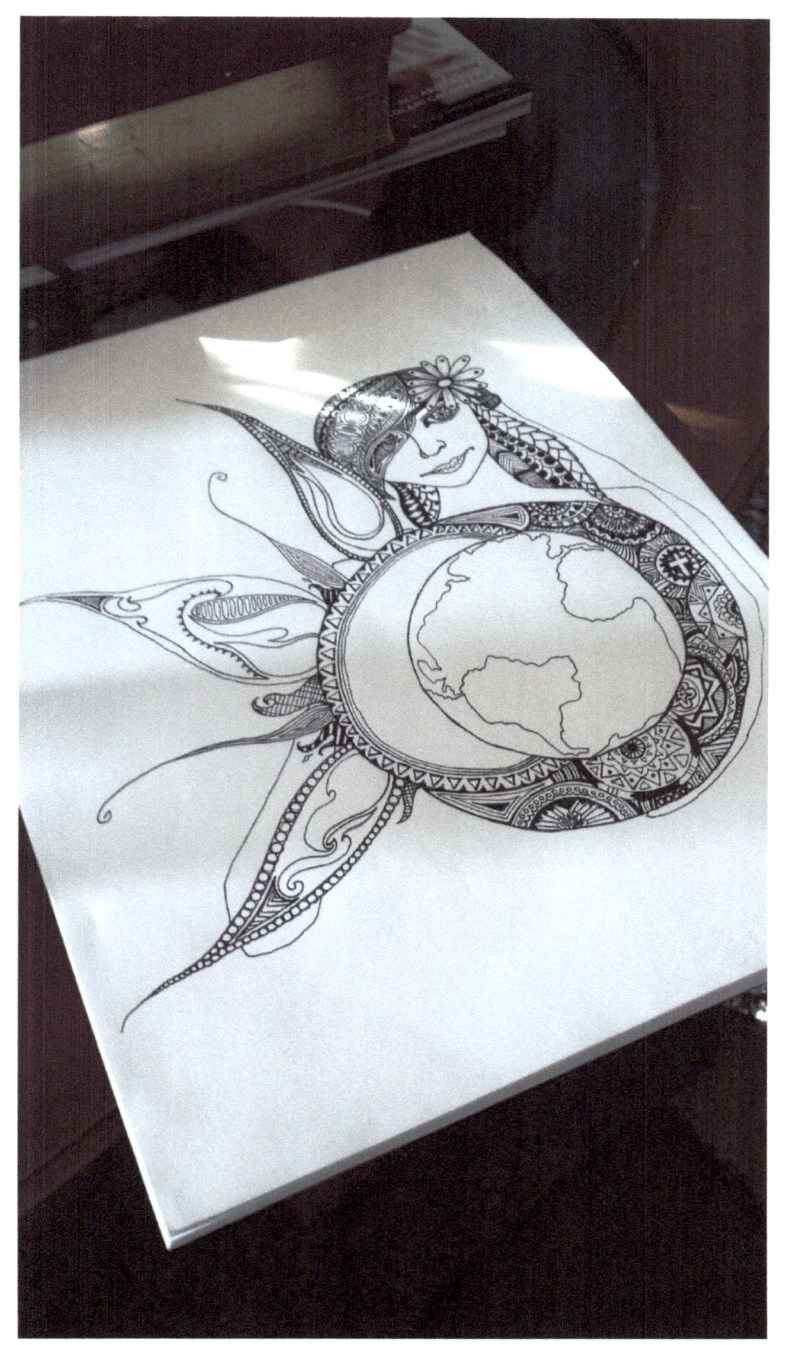

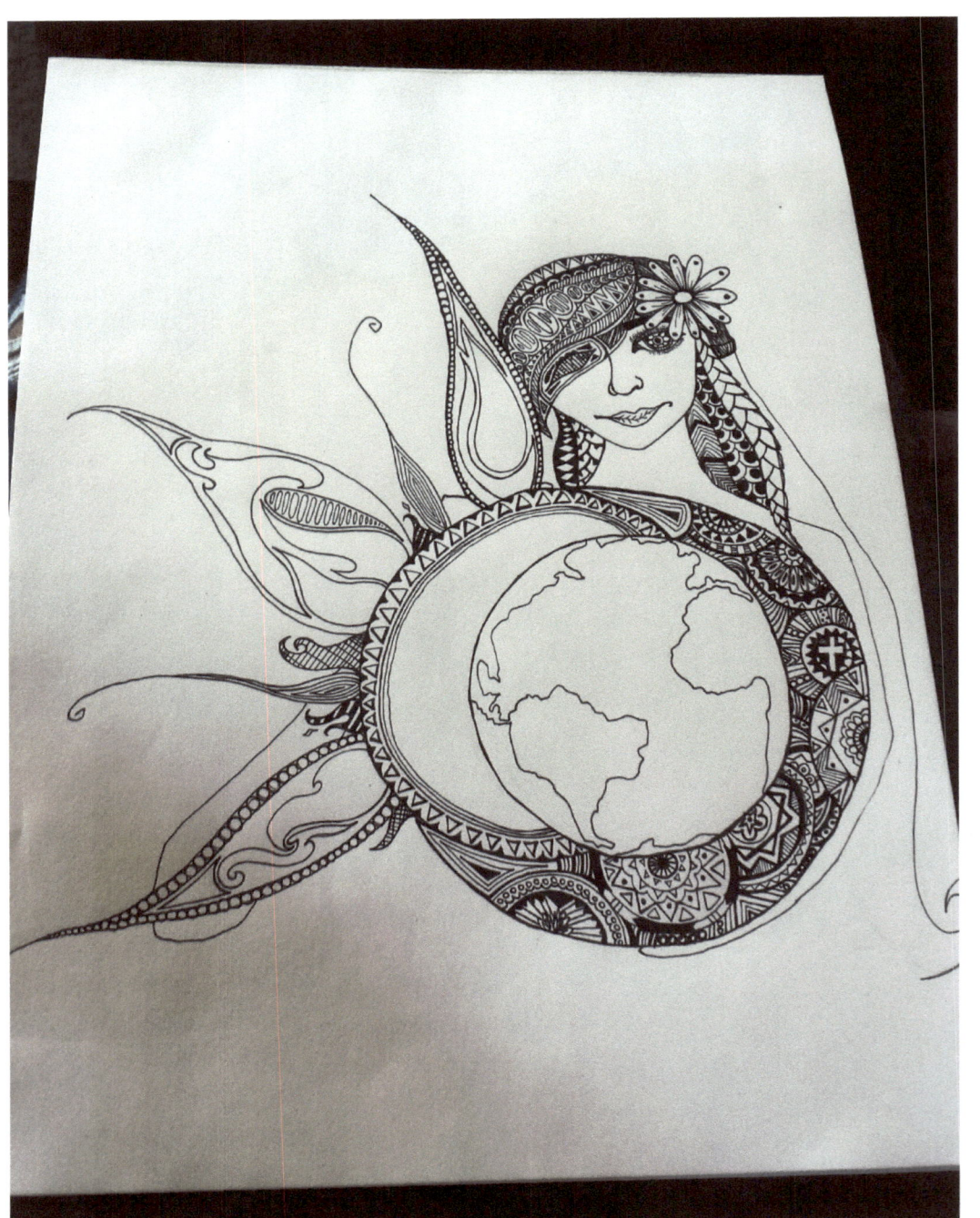

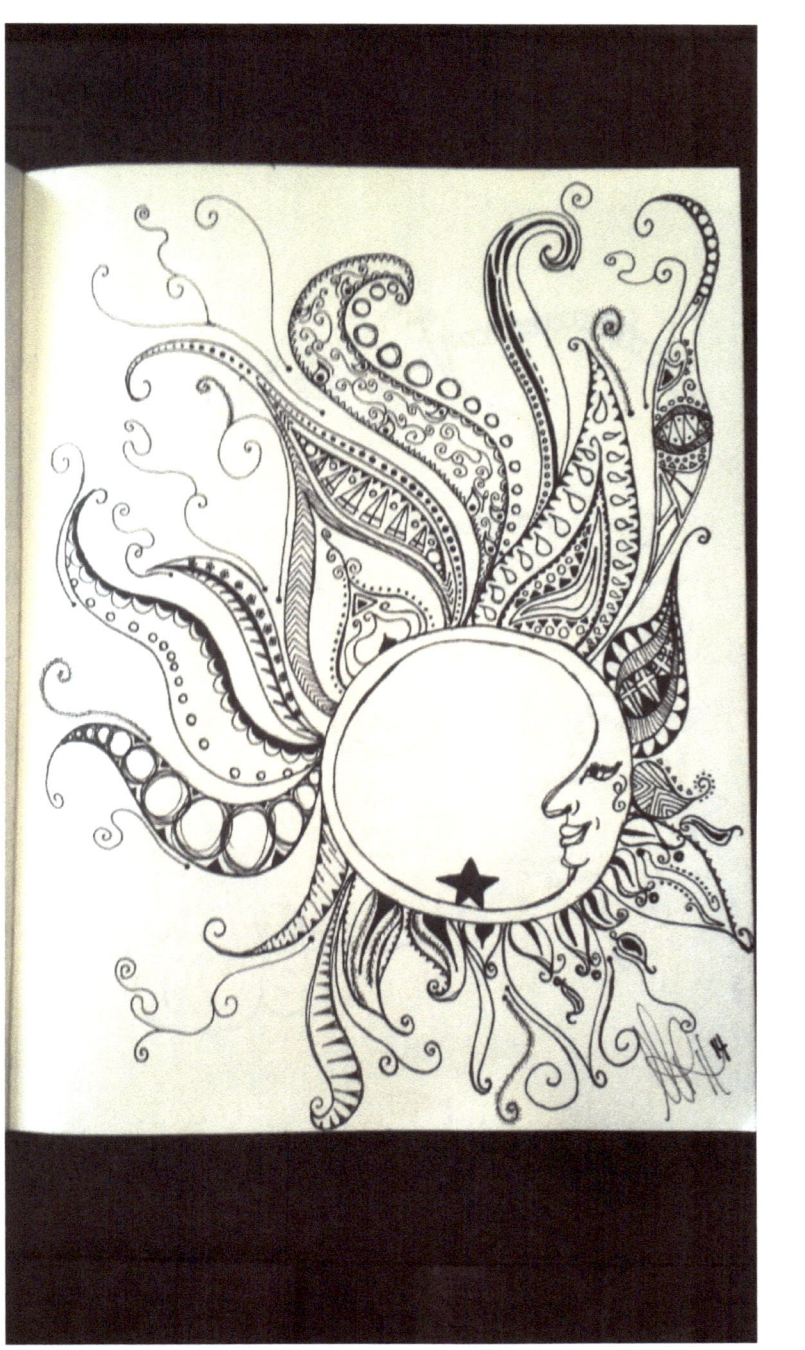

Beautiful -

It's been two years
two years in the making of life without you
It's not easy.
being sad is not a joyous task
life without you
is not a joyous task.
every thought of you pulls harder on my heart strings and
I'm bound to break any moment.
every moment you're not here,
I feel myself becoming more quiet,
more down,
more emotional more depressed more stricken with fear
that I will never get to see your smiling faces ever again.
with you time was of no existence
without you time can't stay away
it ticks and ticks and is just waiting for me to explode
because I can't bear the pressure of your absence.
it's not easy.
easy's not meant to be.

but it would be nice to get a sign every once in awhile saying you're okay saying you are watching me saying you love me or that you miss me too...
no, it's not easy.
it's not easy to forget how you left.
painfully
but eagerly and I don't blame you
the second your heart started to give out your moments were numbered
I relive that day like it was just yesterday
like just yesterday you fought with all your strength to look at me and respond to my weak, crying heart
as yours became more and more weak itself.
I won't ever forget the warm love I saw in your eyes and felt in your hand.
the love I felt in your hand. Though the warmth slipped away never to return.
no, I won't forget.

I won't forget grandma either
her sense of humor
her love
her hugs
her criticism
her painful last days
I could barely even say goodbye
I was so emotional and pained to see her the way she was
frail and in her own kinds of unbearable pain as she
weakened while each second passed.
nothing has been easy.
look up the word sad and you'll find me
look up the word inspirational or unforgettable and you'll
see yourself.
I'm sad because I'm selfish.
selfish for you and the love the two of you shared with me.
you aren't here to see me graduate or get married or
just...anything.
you just aren't here
its not easy.

it will never be easy
but you'll always be beautiful
beautiful like a bird of paradise
don't stay grounded though
open your wings and soar
a beautiful bird like you is not meant to stay in one place
forever.
you have bugger and better things to see and do now that
you aren't living a life of pain
I'm selfish for your love and it's not easy to let go
but if you truly love something, you have to let it go.

MH

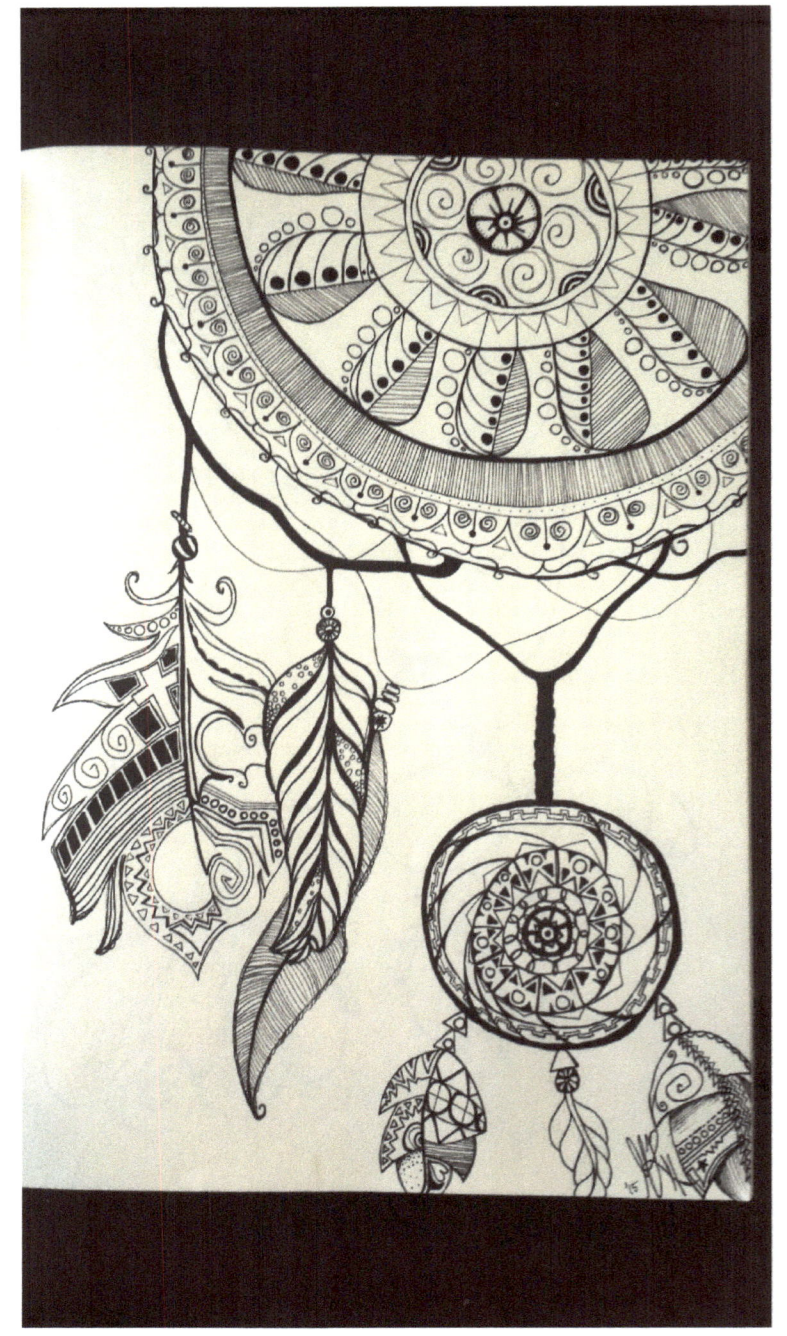

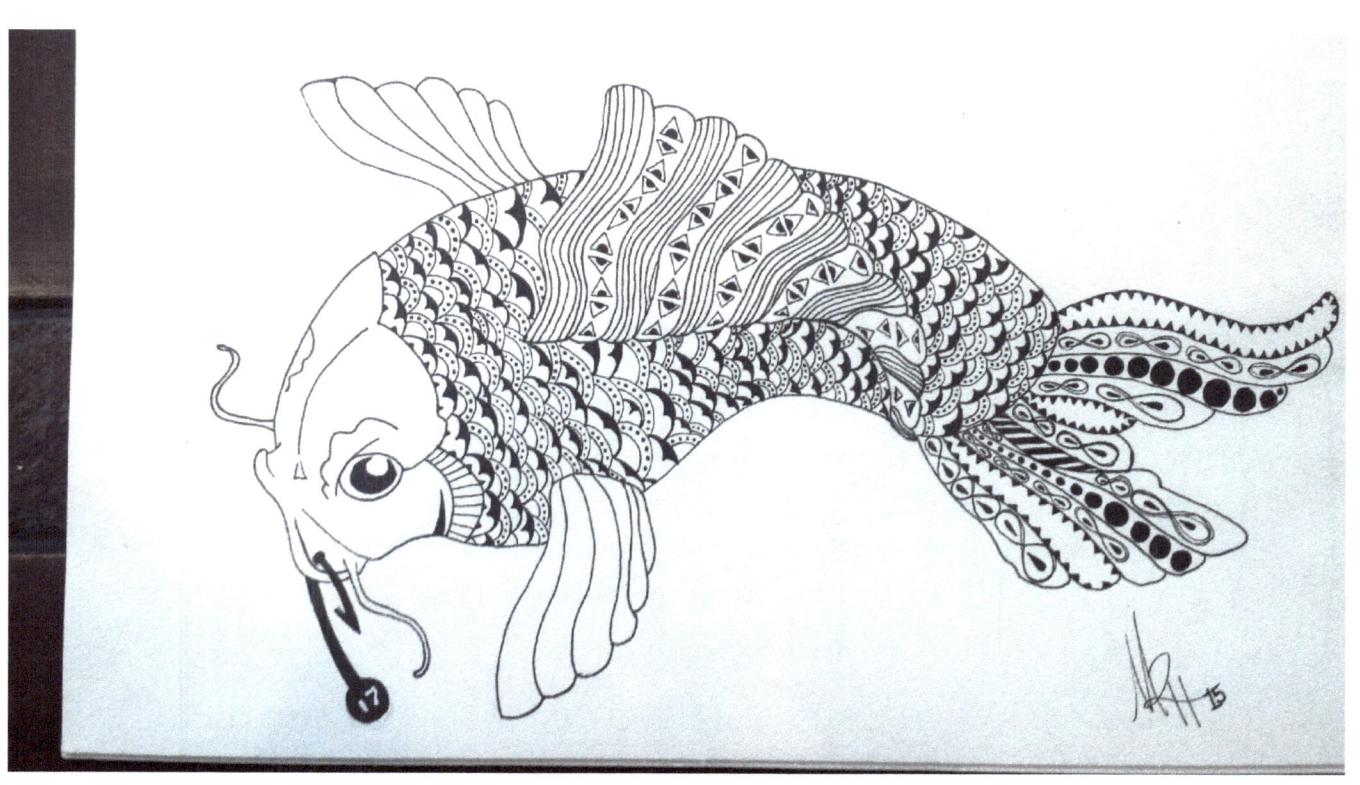

ABOUT THE AUTHOR

Born in Petaluma, California during the early 1970's, Bradley Zink grew up with a passion for books. Instilled in him by his parents, and surrounded with a library of books by Dr. Seuss, Mark Twain and Charles Dickens, to name a few, he developed a true passion for reading. After the birth of his son, Alex, and being a stay-at-home dad, he too instilled the power of reading in his son, too. Using Dr. Seuss as the building blocks for teaching him, Bradley aspired to create a book for Alex, and all children to enjoy. With his son as his muse and inspiration, Bradley is constantly testing out his writings on the world's harshest critic, his son Alex.

www.ingramcontent.com/pod-product-compliance
Lightning Source LLC
Chambersburg PA
CBHW050423180526
45159CB00005B/2394